Waiting for July

K. Scott Fuchs

Published by K. Scott Fuchs, 2024.

WAITING FOR JULY

First edition. September 14, 2024.

Copyright © 2024 K. Scott Fuchs.

ISBN: 979-8227980977

Written by K. Scott Fuchs.

Table of Contents

Dedicated to The Lord Jesus Christ for your love, grace, and many mercies.

Also dedicated to my father, Bill with love and appreciation for the blessing you are.

With special thanks to you the reader with thanks for taking in my work.

WAITING FOR JULY

K. SCOTT FUCHS

Chasing The Wind

How was your day? I am unsure of what to say -
It's not just another head cold,
Another lump of coal, gift wrapped with a bow
Lead me to nothing again,
Confuse with me fairy tale conclusions which are just pretend -
By now it seems only others have use for it.
I haven't seen you in a while,
And if you came back around
I would celebrate!
But you wouldn't notice me in the first place!
A period on a page held up to a galaxy in an expansion state;
A mansion beset in a labyrinth or a cage.
The contrast is not so distinct in an early stage.
It's not another head cold, it's a line gone straight -
With no pulse or rhythm to circulate.
Can you keep your lips pressed to my cheek?
So, I know you'll be here next week;
May I breathe like I once did?
Or is it too late to remember?

Boundary Stone

There is a warmth in the air
A gradient of hope underscored by a feeling of a dread.
Sunrise disguised as a setting sun,
Silhouettes and shadows in the intermediary,
A bubbling brook meandering unto a fleeting tributary.
Chasm to chasm, there is a summit in between
While in reality, the only way to go is down.
When morning light cascades in through the windows,
Grazing under a duvet, locked in the guest room,
As the kids go out and play,
Stomachs ache with failure to access the exit-lane.
An overwhelming urge to lay,
A gurgling surge to waste -
Another precious day.
I don't want to be your enemy,
Only want you to be, my friend.
But as of lately, I been going crazy
Like a Belisha Beacon flashing,
Whilst none dare dash across the street -
Nor walk without reason.
Stuck in this solitary world
Without any boundary stone...

Thank You Dearest Friend

Have I said thank you lately?
For I have curled my fist
And thrown a fit,
Smashed a brick
And latched blades to wrist
Scratching an itch
To stab and slash my ribs
In retaliation for a momentary blip.
And you sat through all sorts of incidents
Still you stood beside me, not bothered, in spite of it.
I appreciate you listening
And giving me space to speak
You never once told me get on with it,
Or keep it brief
Forbearance and patience in abundance
The cord on the rope never severed beneath me,
I did not drown in the wicked seas,
Entangled and ensnared, no plummet to the ground,
Snapping my neck without any muffle of sound.
You wrapped the knot around your finger
And coaxed my hand off the trigger,
Disaster averted with reassurance profound.
Thank you, dearest friend, for watching over me again.

Aisle Nine

In Aisle Nine,
He places cereal on shelves,
In love with life,
Until a quarter to twelve.
It was mid-July
And the skies were blue.
He said stay true to whatever you do,
Love what you make and all will come soon.
Years after the mosh pits in the basements in Franklin Square,
Or driving down Hempstead Avenue listening to the tunes,
With the window down, blowing cigarette smoke in fumes,
I am in a far-away place, thinking of you.
In a supermarket, after hours,
Philosophizing as you organize Fruit Loops
Golden Grahams and candy yams,
Never forgetting the stickball games behind Delaney School.
When I was more optimistic in youth.

A Lake of Fire

If I had to choose a way to die,
It'd be to bathe in a lake of fire!
Whilst moments before, grazing my lover's thigh,
Gazing in to her eyes, as I ache and tire.
Further fatigued, drowsy and sleepy.
To kiss her once more as I commute,
To greet my fate, a glorious blaze absolute.
I'll dive in to the fiery breach
Beneath the sea of silky white sheets
To hold my amore close to me,
As she smiles with felicity, her long auburn hair,
Cerulean eyes that match skies with her skin so fair,
Where it'll forever be, my beloved and me.
No, I would not relent and sound no retreat!
It'd be a dream to die a warrior's death
To taste her love in my last breath.

Why Be in The Majority?

You say you are ahead of the curve,
But you already have struck out.
You state that you are bound to your word,
Mumbling from both corners of your mouth.
You boast that you can ignite the fires,
When you previously snuffed them out;
The more you claim you different,
the more you appear the same.
The brightest smiles
Cannot conceal darkest intent,
All the make-up in the world,
Could not camouflage an ugly heart.
You can put on your nicest dress,
Soak in perfume, and flaunt your breasts.
Wax your legs, and get them all to beg,
But I didn't come here to join the queue,
To spent in a ceaseless cycle of your abuse,
There are so many other things I can do,
Then be faced down in a puddle of puke,
After committing an evening to impress you!
You say you are ahead of the curve,
But you already have struck out,
You state that you are bound to your word,
Mumbling from both corners of your mouth,
You boast that you can ignite the fires,
When you have previously snuffed them out,
The more you claim you different,
the more you appear the same.
You say practice what you preach,
Strictly within an arm's reach.

You state life is a beach,
But only the facts, we should teach!
It's the flavour of the week,
Until it's your turn to speak.
Then you vomit from caprice,
And sneak off into the crease.
Sex sells, but feelings don't pay the rent,
I wonder what is the next idiom, you will implement,
The tricks of the trade, the clues that will cue;
The very ties that bind, you decline that they apply,
Read the fine print, the message resides in between the lines,
I do what I love, and love what I do,
That's why I don't give a hoot, if you a cute because I am obtuse!
The brightest smiles
Cannot conceal darkest intent,
All the make-up in the world,
Could not camouflage an ugly heart.
You say you are ahead of the curve,
But you already have struck out.
You state that you are bound to your word,
Mumbling from both corners of your mouth.
You boast that you can ignite the fires,
When you previously snuffed them out;
The more you claim you different,
the more you appear the same.

Discourses on the American Healthcare System

They raised the cost of an epi-pen
by four hundred forty percent,
Where are the patriots to dissent?
As they raise medical prices and further descend
In to the Land of the Free's variety of Social Darwinism
And unique blend of tyranny
Don't tell me health care is a privilege
When you don't suffer from any given condition,
You don't know what it's like to be faced with over a G for a vial of insulin,
Or to be a parent hearing cancer is afflicting your children,
How they going to flip the bill, even when they have insurance,
Are you picking up the tab and offering any assurance?
No, because it's plenty, rates raise over twenty K
And by the grace of God you don't have to pay,
You live a life free of major sickness
And you have the audacity to condescend anyone with an illness?
Maybe you feel impervious because you have your riches,
Where you have to resort to eBay to sell your britches
To cover the cost of a set of stiches....
Don't call yourself a Christian, forget about forgiveness
You lack compassion, it's apparent your nothing more than a parrot
Not an eagle...
Regurgitating the words of each and every weasel
Spreading fibs, bearing false witness, committing perjuries
Specialists preparing prescriptions in the surgery
They get a bigger hit off the commission, these hypocrites
Forgot about the Hippocratic Oath, the snot flowing out of the nose

In the form of democratic gloats, I hope to expose them in prose
A den of jackals with the hubris and avarice of a pack of goats.
Those who keep defending, please keep on pretending
Systems like the NHS are a farce and communist,
Meanwhile they never read one page of Marx,
Nor one verse in the Bible,
Ultimately, I hope you never find yourself with MS, ALS, Cystic Fibrosis
or Fibromyalgia,
It's no mild asthma, the victims held under a knife and have to pay for
that too.

Lonnie Lane

I knew a fellow named Lonnie Lane,
On Sunday morning, he complained
When a brother came running toward his door
As he smeared cream cheese on his bagel,
He screamed and jeered his car was disabled,
Flames were pouring out from the core,
The engine block under the hood,
Frantic! The passengers sprinted across the neighbourhood,
Bottlenecked in the cul-de-sacs
Decorated with tree-lined verges and split-level ranches,
Green lawns pristinely kept though occasional broken branches.
As for me, he called me to the scene,
To jump the battery,
I asked carefully, are you sure it's not the alternator?
No, no, I am certain
Be cautious be that you are operating close to the radiator,
There is a coolant leak that is indiscrete,
But I need a boost so I can hurry to Chucky Cheese,
Assuredly, I agreed.
As chaos broke out,
I maintained composure,
I opened the trunk to grab a two-litre bottle of H20
To douse the fire before it got out of control.
All the while, he slithered across front yards
Like a crocodile in pursuit of his next meal,
Dude, turn the SUV off, it's not a big deal!
Then Lonnie Lane had a laugh,
Go get a box of Lucky Charms for cereal,
You clearly found a four-leaf clover,
Now I'm going back to check the Yankee game before it's over.

I sighed and replied
Yo homeboy, I am a Mets fan though.
Deadass bro, I am not screwing with ya.

Warning Signs

It's too late now, I can't go on....
I have nothing to live for, what's the use?
I'm tired of life and there is nothing left to do.
I am at the end of my rope, there is no hope...
This is the scope of the trope of those that can't cope;
Forced to mope and grope a lump in their throat, the size of a goat -
Tears running dry in to an endless moat.
I've been feeling identical mentally, so I composed a note...
Perhaps, now you can understand how I truly felt -
What if I don't want any help?
I no longer have to feel by myself
Living the rest of my life,
Like a forgotten ornament rotting on a shelf!
When the blood is splattered where I knelt,
I'd be deceased in a lavatory toilet,
So, let me spill my guts and spoil the ending -
All I ever wanted was to be happy.

Willow Street

On Willow Street,
Through the window breeze,
The dearly deceased,
Lies on pillows in peace,
Outside its nearly eighty degrees.
The neighbours mowed their lawns,
Perhaps had a yawn as they gazed
In the sultry humidity of West Hempstead
Just after dawn.
The smell of death, pungent in the apartment at the third floor,
A scene of serenity and blasphemy hidden to the eyes behind a closed
door.
The pathway seemed like a stairway to heaven -
For he lied on his bed with his eye on the prize,
Somewhere better than may appear in the sky,
Beyond being trapped inside his head.
A collector of firearms, the rifle was appropriate memoranda
To the impromptu mutiny against the commander,
The dictator which controlled his soul,
The one that sold him the fibs that scared him to grow old,
That pulverized him into submission that he dreaded being bold.
I know, my friend, you drove the cab at Rath Park, near the basketball
court in Elmont
Pulled over had a smoke but the TLC stung you at LaGuardia Airport,
as you left for Tremont.
The six-hundred-dollar debt caused you to push harder on that credit
card
And the interest rates accumulated at a pace where you couldn't keep up,
not even a trace.

Frightening you to forsake the chance to move to Texas or Missouri and
pursue the CDL,
So, you got your hustle on and flipped ecstasy until your business acumen
propelled.
And when you decided to French kiss the shotgun shell,
The kiss of death had an embrace that cannot be dispelled.

Dear Tranquillity

Dear Tranquillity,
Why do you flee from me?
I always want to sleep but I awake in a frenzy,
Chest bursting with an ache that twist and digs...
I cannot catch my breath.
Tranquillity, why do you leave me with no peace?
Where my soul feels as if it were on lease,
I stroll down the street –
Looking up to the lights,
Hoping to find relief.
Dearest tranquillity, won't you find me please....
To take away all this pain within me.

Morose Decay in Bethpage

At a 7-Eleven in Bethpage
Mid-way between Stewart Avenue and Hicksville Road,
I erode in my Dodge as I sip on my coffee
With Vanilla Butter Toffee creamer for ninety-nine cents.
It doesn't make sense,
I contemplate and commiserate.
Listless in a parking space,
In the winter of 2008.
A decade has gone since - a daydream of today.
Looking back to this place,
Where it was all in front of me, there was something to chase.
Before the fleeting feeling of being at the end of the race.
Listening to the *Futures* album on repeat -
Sprawling against the cloth upholstery,
As I remain in idle, blaring the heat,
Slurping my coffee, searching for a moment of peace.

Embarkation Upon the Central Line

London, England
The one I love, singing
She is beautiful!
Ravens Row forget me
Wandering the street aimlessly
Stepping in history.
Wells Mews
If they only knew what
You been through
In the greenery,
Regents Park reminds me of
Beauty's simplicity

Meditations in Green Park

In a preserve, I observed how it was pleasant.
Perturbed with discontent, I solicited a question.
Is love an apparition, a mirage in the desert?
Or reserved for those who don't deserve it or get it?

Sandbox Rules Over A Game of Pool

You speak of the distance you've travelled,
But ignore where I have tread;
And when I try to show you,
You claim, it's all in my head!
It's easier to argue, more difficult to peruse -
But we could be swapping shoes depending on where we fell in the queue...
Place me in a box,
Affix a label to the top.
Fit me in your pocket,
There is no incentive to stop -
Apply your analytics,
Render your metrics astute,
When asked to dive deeper,
You reply, it's no longer planned for review
A panorama of paraphernalia,
For a pantomime that is a flailing azalea.
You speak of the distance you've travelled,
But ignore where I have tread;
And when I try to show you,
You claim it's all in my head!
It's easier to argue, more difficult to peruse -
But we could be swapping shoes depending on where we fell in the queue...
Cleave to your fabrications
They are your only source and proof
When you are educated or forewarned,
You remain steadfast and aloof -
You can cease to wrinkle your nose -
Or smirk back crudely too -

The essence of uncovering knowledge,
Discovering what to deduce,
In actuality which is true.

Nicole and Hollie Are on The Bar

For some it's a ritual,
But me, it's never trivial,
Back against the wall,
As all the shades of light cascade,
The ladies raze on the stage.
I gaze from a distance,
As they radiate the prism,
Evading the prison that encroaches on my disposition.
To me I am no different than the magpie perched high above,
On the ceiling of the flat,
They can't touch me, yet...
But they don't see me anything more than a pest.
They go in there every Friday
Indulging in their cocktails, sharing tales
From the week that has assailed,
Debuting their stylish clothes,
Filleting psychology, so they can be enclosed
In a bubble amongst their peers,
Whilst I am just some guy, that's weird.
Malingering somewhere in the tiers.
If I establish eye contact,
Approach with tact,
With the aspiration of conversation,
I balked as you walk to your ultimate destination.
For me, it was you,
But for you, I was never a spec on the screen,
A blip on the radar from a far,
No proximity or anywhere in between.

A Dispute in Highbury

"The Gunners plays with passion and grit, you supercilious git!"
I reply, "You are a Stunner",
I lay in a mansion covered in shit.
A delirious twit you plundered and miss.
Under roars of thunder, I envision a summer of bliss,
Where you and I are together sharing a kiss.
I love the Bulldogs, I cheer each and every Saturday,
But I'd never let anything separate you and me –
As you proclaim *"It's a tom-tit, a Wallace and Gromit"*
In my opinion, 'it's more poignant to keep your promise."
I can write discourses and sonnets
About your chocolate-coloured bonnet.
The thought of you with another lover,
I cannot stomach...
It forces me to cough and vomit.
"Arsenal amazes in fashion,
Yet the Gunners do not quit."

Sour Blue Bon Bons

Confections first taste sweet against the tongue,
Until the bitterness comes, as one savours the texture.
The pangs of citron and the zest of raspberry,
Calamity disguised beneath a captivating display -
She curls her hair,
Brews up a cup of Yorkshire tea,
Then transitions to stronger stuff,
Vis-a-vie., vodka, gin, and whisky.
She sings as if it were karaoke,
Mimicking JT, she just wants to pirouette and forget -
Indeed, there is something magical,
It's fete in the air, and she can put her finger on it.
Verily, it will be her cell phone
At three-in-the morning when she is drunk,
A temper-tantrum at random for whatever,
Stewing in the back of her cranium.
She'll do it when I am alone and asleep,
When my vulnerability is at its peak.
Because she is angry, she has two children
With two different lowlifes who didn't treat her right,
And she spent years with a guy
Who slept until two in the afternoon,
Whilst she went to work.
But don't you know that's not me?
I am light on my feet, filled with effervescent energy
We can bump and grind,
Fuck each other blind,
But she rather dump, and find
A reason to give her axe a grind.

A Chalice of Champagne

It's all fun and games,
Until the joke is on you,
You laugh and call me lame,
It's all too easy for you...
I am the one that you blame,
For the milk you spilled, without further ado.
You won't even refer to me, by my name,
That's just not the cool thing to do.
Recline in your chaise in the corner of your lounge,
Slurp on some ciders, then cast a frown!
Go on and tell you don't care, when truly you can't handle what you feel
But me, this is no trick, I always try to be real,
I leave no stone unturned; my gun is not hidden -
Shooting straight from the hip, so the point is not missed when,
The pebbles in the shoes provide hindrance.
Pour out a chalice of champagne for a pint of piss,
Make a sour face when you taste your own bitterness.
Spray a steady stream of mace, then toss the buck,
Label me a disgrace, and state I was never good enough.

Disparate and Desperate – Closer Than a Vowel

You are a pro at giving the cold shoulder -
Smouldering embers, frozen over.
Was it something I said?
Anything I did?
Insert contractions, pronouns, and adjectives
And don't forget to ad-lib.

Being Duplicitous is a Dangerous Thing

Being duplicitous can be dangerous;
It can be construed as contiguous and become contagious,
Apportioned to the norm -
Acting deceitful can cause peril and harm,
Especially when it is understood to be next in sequence and calm -
Regularly accepted by many as practical, not wrong.

The Man in The Phone Booth

I've always been the man the phone in the booth,
On a lonely corner, along a desolate street;
Enclosed in between panes of glass that encase me with a paltry blanket,
Which smothers me with haste.
Frustration and despair, impairs my cognition.
I bludgeon the receptor against the holster, forging incisions.
Over and over until the fixture is broken -
As nuts and bolts disintegrate in to battered components.
The broken pieces and fragmented remains,
Ricochet off the carved scratches and imperfections,
In chaos and calamity,
I shattered the surface, billowing down the littered footpath,
A bath of scattered shards of glass
Ravishing in the lavish release of wrath.
From the sulking taverns and musky theatres.
There's a million ways to draw a circle, but none of them are right
But me, I am the hypotenuse of a triangle, begging to be right.
Falling and falling away from sight.
I'll never be in the vertex, nestled and tight,
Forever, dragged parallel in congruence,
The form of the plight!
Yes, I rejoice and bellow in the phone booth, because I am finally free!
Maybe now, you will finally, listen to me!

The Philosopher of the Beer Garden

The philosopher of the beer garden;
The preacher upon a bar stool;
The leader glued to the couch.
The one who pens overtures;
Who envisions money in his mind;
That appears with the push of a button on a tablet.
Blockchain technology is not the root cause;
Data analytics are not the play after the pause;
Articulating thoughts without opening their mouth.
I sat there with a pint of Budweiser;
Taking heavy drags of a Marlboro;
After ingesting a bag of Haribo;
Though my analogies never made me wiser.
I have the schematic and plan of action;
Each step manufactured with objectives unravelling;
But it didn't happen, because none could manage;
With what I was telling them.
Yet it is so compelling then,
So, I went home, vented my frustration
In between these sentences after studying mathematical equations.
You would never know of me,
Nor do I ever matter, in the final affirmation.

S.I.S.

Wish in one hand or shit in another,
See which of the two fills up quicker -
It doesn't matter whether it's last night's steak and lobster
Or a stewed bowl of gruel -
Whether you had loose stools or nuggets of poop upon the next afternoon
It comes from the same location onward to identical destinations -
You can dare compare and contrast,
I'll sit back there and laugh,
Comb my hair and take a bath -
Remove your skull from the cistern, get your head out of the latrine
Mull over the concern instead to getting clean
You can dress it up with a bow, if you prefer
But shit is shit and all one can do is acquiesce and conquer.

Between the Hedgerows

Beyond the boundary,
In between the chalk lines -
There is serenity in the madness
Distractions glancing onward, dare not enter.
Shift to focus on the task at hand,
That which assembles in the front, at center.
And in this clarity, there are no disparities.
No longer is there a need to introspect, concerning before and after -
Unless an opponent impedes the gap, then tackle whatever moves.

Tuppence for Your Thoughts

You can pick or spare
Hairs from the back of your napes,
Irrespective of size and shape,
Like you have unlimited Nair
The sustenance to sustain -
Whilst debonair like Nature Boy Ric Flair
Carousing Devon Air,
Cruise, levitate, and then raise
The stakes if you dare.
All in with Frosted Flakes, in exchange for a baseball steak
An uneven trade, results of the poker game.
Caught bluffing with a muffin against a full straight,
When you had nothing more than a Jack and an Eight!
With an Ace of spades, staring back at you as you vape.
And no homily can remedy which humiliates, nor abate the hate the permeates further,
And firmly resonates!
Like squeaking breaks in the pouring rain,
Stop, pump, and check the pads and plates,
Then carry on forward, do not hesitate!
But I cannot command you where or not you dance around or prance about
The parking lot or car park in leather pants and clogs,
Only advise you of the spectacle,
Coinciding with the subsequent thoughts.

Maisie

On Christmas eve,
She sat by the chimney,
Brushing aside leaves
Collected from the Heath.
The fire crackling,
She licked her teeth,
Waiting for a piece
Of minced roast beef.
She giggles as snow falls on the street,
With no interest of shovelling the sleet,
She hurries to sleep,
On Christmas eve.
In Manchester, past a century.
Maisie directs me to a land of make believe,
Every time I nap in the terraced house,
Where she used to be.

Hully's Poem

What he said,
Can be deduced.
On the subject of statuses and haikus.
It is true,
What he has stated and said
There is proof!
Five syllables
Followed by seven.
Is the formula.
I am not warning you -
Nor taunting ya,
Or making a fool!
You must break through
The rubric
Before it comes and gets you!

The Kitchen Sink

You can't throw the baby out with the bathwater
A ton of bricks versus a ton of feathers,
Weighed upon a scale and measure.
A mix of good and bad comether.
The mirage that one can tip the gavel
Confirmed by the compulsion of either,
Venn diagrams ascribed in ether.
Upon termination, there are no tethers
In the end, all things come equal –
Those lines will blur together.

En Espanol

Nunca necessita usar palabras, para la poesia.
Solamente uso por una pobrecita.
Ella, que linda! y que bonita!
Pero pierde grande y gana poquita.
Entonce yo deseo escribir un articulo,
Como Ella puede leer que se amo.

A Right Royal Knees-Up

The notions are voluminous,
Potent as the ocean.
But the ideas aren't flowing;
Just stuck frozen, staring at an open notebook,
Whilst composing a new poem.
Out on the streets, there is jubilee, all make merry
But I am inside, fixating on my blank page.
Because none will subside, until I've written a line,
Word by word, phrase by phrase!
I cannot elate, until I forge and innovate -
Come forth, when I create.
Shake off the writer's block,
And stop the perpetuating an imperfect circle
Which paradoxically, defines no correlation.
I call my man Caster up in Lancaster,
We shared a laugh and had some banter -
Making light of the disaster.
While the poetry flows through me,
I reprise and revise the latest chapters,
Like riding a sleigh, without Dasher and Prancer.

The Girl with The Biblical Name

By golly,
The girl with the biblical name standing outside Molly's!
I was about to get on the stage, but she is looking quite dolly.
I couldn't perform, but alas thus is quite the norm,
For a mister to delight in his brother's sister.
Yes! I would love to get with her, my affections -
building like a blister.
How I could see, me as a sitter for her four children,
When she out doing errands,
And I am at home, cooking her a dinner.
I hold no intentions of a sinner
No, I want to go off a winner!
To make her happy and render,
Some of her pressures thinner.
Couples are supposed to take care of stuff together,
For worse or for better,
I want to be her, go-getter.

Georgianna Marie

Georgianna Marie
Skipped by, eating a pear,
As she reprieved from weaving baskets of potpourri.
She smiled gently and nodded discretely
I was sitting on the steps
Perplexed, until she greeted me
"You appear to have much to get off your chest?"
She flicked off her hat and let down her hair
Chuckled and grasped my fingers
Don't let this linger, she said
Seize the opportunity, for it may never come round again!
I'll tell you once more my friend,
Seize the opportunity, don't you dare have fear
Envision it as much as you did, but its finally here!
It appeared in a hurry; you could never be prepared.
Why shy away?
Like a blue jay perched on a branch
It can fly away, if you take your eye off the chance.
Verily, you have been sitting outside
Sitting under the tree, patiently
Awaiting me, so why you pacing, peach?
Take hold of me and let us run off together....

Read Between The Lines

1. I think it's comedic when the adverts are raving
2. About how some agency can enhance your savings.
3. Both time and money placed back in your pocket.
4. Time is money, but I am no prophet.
5. Is a timeline, a calendar of profits?
6. I can spot it!
7. For values are imaginary, all speculatory and projected
8. Socially as a community we accept it.
9. If we reject it, can we re-assign the MSRP?
10. Or do we simply let it be?
11. The GDP is an inaccurate algorithm of the economy,
12. Because there is no commerce in autonomy.
13. It's an automatic rehearsed mercantile philosophy,
14. That we simply accept as normality.
15. I'll toss out the idioms about the grass too high -
16. And the serpents lurking serpentine,
17. On a porcelain slide in to their girth of wine.
18. No! I'll just pretend everything is peachy and sublime,
19. When I see some cute advertisement with a catchy rhyme.

Dirty Dishes

You stood in the kitchen, scrubbing plates merrily.
A Batman towel tied around your neck,
As you rinsed the bowls, cleansing each and every speck.
It was 2:30 the morning, I was yawning, you disclosed you felt a tad sick.
I offered to exit, so you can rest and catch up on sleep,
Politely, you responded 'Darling you need not leave"
Gently, I stroked her scalp, drowsy she became, I left thirty minutes early.
She jeered 'Well we have the rest of eternity to spend together'
I simpered 'Exactly, a half hour won't kill me'
She chuckled and kissed me goodnight,
I trekked onward under the cover of fluorescent LED streetlights.
Making my way down Smallshaw Lane, only to await paltry raw pain.
How could you wash up so indiscriminately?
Tell me you love me than simply forget me?

The Lily in Thorns

In a field lies a white lily surrounded by thorns,
Sardonically mocking me, her object of scorn.
This lily is more beautiful than all the rest,
Silky and plush with cream-colored breasts.
Never have I seen such a botany, so lovely,
Shining with grandeur, a marvellous spectacle.
I would gladly draw my own blood, reaching through the brier,
To hold the lily, smell the fragrance, and admire.
I would sever arteries and slice my veins,
If it cost me everything, the price would not be in vain.
I would walk across fire, swim through the seas,
For this beautiful lily to simply love me.

A Fly in a Jar

Words revealed,
Beauty concealed;
Are they even real?
She is a candle,
Lighting up the room.
Approach too close,
Your fingers singed soon.
But I am a fly stuck in a jar,
Admiring her radiance from a far;
Praying, that I can bathe in her warmth.

Thank You – II

From the chrysalis, spawn butterflies
Drawn from caterpillar larvae,
As soil rots away, to give way to new flowers, this May
You too washed a way through my dismay.
What was once a day of infamy
Now, a holiday of triumph
Only you could steer the change,
Thank you –

Euphonic Musings

If I wished for my death
Then I would not get
A chance to change events
I could not forget.
Tears which were wept.

For the Dawgs

The moment has arrived to settle accounts!
To dig cleats in to the mound and squabble in bouts!
To challenge the lot of injustices and surmount!
To struggle and tussle, rumble and fight!
To never back down!

An Incident Near The Arndale

Slithering sidewalk serpents
Screaming salacious soliloquies
Stared at me subliminally diving expediently in the trajectory of the
machinery
Commandeered effectively in the sleet.
The shape of the scheme;
A soldier of the spirit, a son of the street with a shoulder of spearmint.
A solder in Spherion with a succulent stash of suckering succotash –
Subsequently suffering splashes of sarsaparilla,
To remedy rashes reversed like a rogue rubella!
So, skip to Skelmersdale to Sir Elmer Dale's sale to requisition direct
conscriptions to wreck the sickness; swap the S for a cheeky C
To curate conspiracies, crawl toward the curb, and cantilever circa a
Camry.
Dilly-dallying completely to the sire steering stiffly
Cocking up the staged sequence like stealth superheroes donning armour
in lieu of lycra and sequins.

An Exhibition on the M60

Two vessels commuting opposite lanes upon a motorway
One passage held at a stand-still whilst another is wide open and bustling
-

A mile or two down past the next junction,
The carriages in antiparallel orientations,
Never crossing at a perpendicular intersection -
What was one's past, is another's future.
One glance from a side-view mirror into what will be seen,
You see, I used to look forward but now I can only turn back –

Along Ashton Old Road

I am always caught glancing over at you -
You are the first thing I look for,
When I step underneath the nave
Looking forward to Sunday morning, hoping you don't go off with
someone else.
Travelling down the Old Road, feeling uplifted and like myself.
Didn't wake up with night sweats,
And the ceiling hasn't dropped yet.
Finally got a good night sleep in,
And the mould is not seeping.
We can go out for coffee,
After the pastor is done preaching.
Let's stroll down the Old Road
And enjoy the rest of Sunday,
Walk on down to the cafe and sit on the swings in Debdale,
Forget the shadows by the sundial and share some tales
Of another's life prior to Manchester;
On the things that drove us both to the centre
And ticks before, I head through Openshaw.
I'll give you a hug with a silly joke, then escort you home -
Not before we stop at the Morrison's
And purchase a couple Rubicons,
Dually noting how you prefer a straw, in the can.
Whilst debating whether to stop and listen to Misty Mountain Hop
or Bron-Y-Aur Stomp.
Didn't have any nightmares,
And the seal around the sink, is still set,
I am truly happy
And I didn't wake yet.

The View from The Chew

A vertigo with no impetus
Haemorrhaging in a brisk.
Cold whisk, pulling in a million different
directions with no objective clearly stated.
Perhaps imagination has faded;
Or maybe yet, the brain is jaded.
It's an errand to put pen to pad -
When you are always mad and stressed, distracted by texts
Fiending for sex, or wondering how you'll be fed next.
Revisions to the project, contactless won't connect,
Credit card payment due on Tuesday;
Onboarding and DBS checks in between every step
After one's barely slept -
It's an A-road through the city centre,
Car engines revving in between idles for attention.
Beats and bass gyrating through speakers,
Complementing the clattering of sneakers.
On the footpath through the traffic,
Pedestrians and gridlock interwoven creating havoc;
When all you want to do is sit alone up in the hills and chill -

Life and Death

Dead and buried;
Buried and dead
Does it matter which way you say it, my friend?
The irony of decades elapsed –
The figure as pictured, beset on a facade of brick
In her day, it was cast iron to support her as she sits.
Black and white colour-scape, five by eight frame
The building remains, unchanged since -
She adjusted her hat, walked off, became married with kids,
And I am standing here, wondering where she has been?
Why I missed her, and if she still even exists?
If only I could have touched her,
To feel the soft skin of her wrist,
How her lips curl against one's cheek
When she greets with a kiss.
To dip one's nose into the nectar of a rose,
Indulge in its sweet aroma, lie in a bed of grass,
And watch the clouds pass -
To hold a gentle hand, and stroll casually down the
cobblestone road,
Could you please, freeze that moment, and never let go?

The 15th of July

These trees weren't here a 100 years ago.
The seeds were long planted before we could fathom.
These streets, the residents may not be the same
As it once was in a previous age;
But the still frame photographs of the houses remain...
The oaks, hawthorn, and birch
Weren't perched to form a canopy,
They were a fraction of their roots
Which sprawl beneath the grassy yards.
Reaching hard to clutch us with hardened bark -
A century ago
A pier once stood at the end,
A grand citadel with all the accoutrements
And amusements, from a bandstand to a carousel,
A day out for the family,
A young woman pushed a pram on that corner of the sand
Now occupied by a man and his friend,
Immersed and absorbed
In thoughts that plunge to the depths,
Submerged beneath the surf
That charges toward the aged jetty.
What did that women think then?
In 1910, when her photograph was taken,
Holding her baby against her, chilled by the breeze, subtly shaking
It was just another day, the 15th of July
Captured there beside us on this very beach.
Toddlers crawl by, fathers sprint for gelato cones,
Mothers fix their focus to their mobile phones, so many basking in the
sun

Yet so many more alone.

The gulls caw, the waves break, a faint sizzle of barbecued steak,

All the while, I had it wrong, but now I sigh, perhaps it can finally be right,

That day by the sea on the 15th of July.

More Poetry About Miss Lee

And this is why, I grovel!
Banging the floorboards with my fists,
Clutching the fabric of your dress.
Hoping, I could somehow taste your faint scent.
Where it's five minutes or 120 years, the distance remains the same,
Perforated edges stay, designating the mark.
Whether you be a mile a field,
Or thousands of kilometres spanning seas,
I always felt you belong to me,
And I to you,
But instead of being early to the wedding,
I am late to my funeral,
Why don't you just bury me?
For I am haunted the imagery,
I see your face in paintings;
Constantly they tell me, you are sick,
Caught and stuck in your own world,
Won't you join us in this reality?
But my vision persistently wanders, to look for you.
For the only existence I want...
Is the one, where I kiss you.

Somewhere in the Middle of Nowhere

There is not much left to write,
Stuck in a block that whirls around in circles.
A triangle formed in a quadrilateral
With vertices fixed at opposing ends.
Mathematically, geometrically, or emotionally empty,
The only point ahead is the one where the lights go off.
Sigh and shut thine eyes for one final time,
And peacefully recline - all will be fine,
All will be fine, once I have left.
Into your arms, I commend my spirit,
Into her embrace, I crave to be held.
A world much different than this once,
A place that doesn't seem to exist.
One filled with peace and bliss,
Where we can all gather together and share good news.
All will be fine, all will be fine,
But we never left, we were meant to be there all along.
A Rubik's cube with no arithmetic to resolve the code,
Deteriorating loaves of bread, crusted in corrode.
My fingers scramble across the cupboard, covered in mould,
A Conestoga Stagecoach in route to calibrate a caliphate
That will serve as a milestone for the underlying roots.
Once I leave, I will return to where I was meant to be.
Looking over my shoulder with sunlight guiding me back to home,
With our noses entrenched in the scent of lavender
As a warm breeze chases us through the botany.
Humming the lyrics of *Revolution Song*, vociferously -
I cannot remember before, nor do I want to, I am busy chasing you to
where we go,
Until we finally find some shade and I rest my head against yours,

Peacefully recline with your heart wrapped in mine -
All will be fine, all will be fine
Finally! I am where I was meant to be...

The Story of a Shirt

Fear not, inscribed in yellow Gothic font.
Luminescent against a black backdrop of angst.
To Blackrod, I travel early to avert being late -
For a first date.
I took it with me, the shirt placed on the seat to remind me,
Fear not, though you have never been here previously.
This could be the start of something new -
What you have longed for, finally come true...
Leave the shirt in the Civic and pivot across to the SPAR whilst it's only
spittin'
Browsing the shelves, watching the clock until our lips will lock.
Meander over the road, halting at the brow, looking out
At the many cars scurrying by on the motorway, miles away,
Unaware I was watching them pass.
Perhaps one motorist glanced back,
Having a laugh, wondering if I was observing from a far.
Though we never met, we shared a moment together -
Like two stars in a sky, hurling through space -
Some never cross paths, whilst others collide.
Like my beloved and I.
I captured her heart as she laid claim to mine.
Days, then weeks, then months elapsed.
The shirt found clasped in the backseat,
Accompanying her and I, to St. Anne's by the Sea;
And the many declarations of I love you to her.
The joy that filled the cabin back and forth
Our intimate moments on the porch, or travelling north towards Wigan
My love,
Shatter my heart
And drive a stake through my spirit.

Abandon me in the wreckage, and tell me you don't want to hear it!
No way to avoid, a void consoled by smokes and spirits
On a main road through Swinley, swindling Budweiser's before breakfast.
Emptying bank accounts into packs of Benson and Hedges Gold's -
Roaming south toward Acton Terrace where the first Uncle Joe's Mint Balls were sold,
Desperately fleeing from the scenes in search of a serenity from these cacophonies.
Load up the hatchback,
Throw the boxes in the boot -
It's time to move -
Lying on the vamp,
The shirt behind a lava lamp,
It made me think of you...
Flushed down the toilet, soaked in the tears that pour,
Left decaying in a room with plywood floors.
An empty kitchen echoing the silence of your absence -
Crusted pots upon a stove with contaminated forks, long forgotten.
And so, another tumbleweed blows across Manchester,
Back to where I was before I met her.
A jar of sauce crashes against the concrete,
Orange mascarpone splashing at my feet,
Remove all the glass shrapnel safely -
Reminding me, that which was elucidated, eludes me.
There in the trunk was the shirt described before,
Collecting all the red chunks and broken pieces,
The itsy-bitsy fragments that left me speechless -
When she destroyed my heart completely,
Wrap the mess in the top and dispose it in a receptacle on the other side of the road,
Alas, a story is told that few may ever know....

A chainmail of poetry and prose, detailing a
Wilted rose whose petals are scattered in the wind.
What began with fireworks, culminates in an unheard whisper.

Written to the Tune of A Movie Kind of Life

Your daughters the ring-bearers, emptying a basket of petals -
That was supposed to be this day back to the then,
I've gone to so many locations but you've stayed where you've been,
A whirlpool of emotions which always bring me back to you -
In route to the chemist, dedicated to pursue
A lifeline, I could peruse -
Such scribblings are imaginations of fiction;
Rehearsed and revised over a lifetime;
Connecting the lines and cadence, making sure they all rhyme.
All I want to do is sit in my bedroom
And write poems about how I don't give a fuck
About giving a fuck.
My methods to cope on this occasion have left abrupt.
You withdrew me from my cocoon,
Struck down in amazement, I wrote you twenty pages of romantic notes.
My soul captured in containment;
A gilded cage, I have no regrets regardless -
Because my sole aspiration is to give you love.
I stand with you hand-in-hand
Your hair down your back, adorned in pearl and laces
The brightest of smiles, elegantly enamelled across porcelain faces.
My methods to cope on this occasion, have left abrupt -
Because all I want to do is sit in my bedroom
And write poems about how I don't give a fuck.
But I could never like you, for it is solely love.
We lie in each other's embraces, I can feel your pulse racing,
Now a window separates us, like we never were acquainted.
My love and mate, I confide in whence it is late and, no one is around,

Now strangers that appear out of place when, everyone's abound.

An Overcast Sky

An overcast sky, gradients of grey, smoke, and charcoal
Billowing down and through wafting white clouds,
A breeze sweeps across an emerald field, glistening between juniper and spring,
As the sunlight grows dim.
The wind roars louder, I hear your name whispered in the gust,
As chimes jingle, branches creak then cringle, before all returns to a hush.
Across the clough, beyond the hidden mud amongst the peat and bog,
Rows of terraced houses with front gardens encroached by oaken picket fences,
Bay windows assorted with a cornucopia of curtains drawn
In a medley of colours like the tops of crayons set in a box.
You reside among the tapestry, the brightest shade of all.
You are so close, yet so far,
Across the green, just beyond the gate -
Your face; your voice; your embrace are landmarks and signposts
Towards moments long ago, which will never come again.
The railway line set on the hill, overlooks the scene
The carriage house pub with a thatched facade at the opposite end of the lane
Remains ignorant to the pain, blissfully unaware of the suffering in the air;
Impervious to the melancholy in all the surroundings;
A midst all the beauty; in the centre of the botany and splendour,
Coal and embers are cast upon a soul, inconsolable and tender.
A broken heart with fragments sprinkled about like the mist that watered the grass of the field -
Your name, cried from quivering lips, trickling down the lane from tears that formed the rain,

Your name, heard once more in the faint wind that blows onward, from the day you were gone.

Veules-les-Roses

Paralysed in blind rage,
Sat in the same place
For two hours gone by
Fingers pressed to six
Digits on the mobile
I am about to break
Misanthropy is swirling through me like chantilly,
I was supposed to recuperate
But I am engrossed, prostrate
In a chair, running my hands through my hair.
No one else is there -
Though I suffocate in a crowded square,
Walls comprised of skull,
Chaos thick in the air.
Synergy pacing through my marrow,
Eyes narrow as I stare.
If only, I could leave,
And journey to your village,
A place for lovers,
Free of plunder and pillage.
We can lie cheek-to-cheek
Hand in hand in the weeds,
And listen on intently
When the other speaks,
Head resting on your belly -
As I drift off to sleep.

Arabesque

Conjecture, I am lost, gone forever,
Lost in your soft complexion,
The rouge applied to your cheeks -
Which accent your fair face;
The shine of your eyes,
And the light which traces...
Your nose, your lips,
And the bows that flair -
From the plaits of your hair.
The wild tapestry of colour and shape,
Auburn to grape, aquamarine to cerulean,
Ivory to magenta, the drapes that careen -
Sensations, once you enter.
As Arabesque reverberates through the crown mouldings,
Under the glass conservatory ceiling,
I notice how your jewellery meshes with the goldenrod satin
of your bodice.
Neatly tucked buttons that contour to your hourglass figure;
The violet overdress which falls downward,
Coinciding with the cascades of hair over your spine.
Why ever ponder death and disease?
When I can stay on you and me,
Dashing across flowery greens.
I can smell the pollen; I can taste the spring!
Distances afield, encapsulated in our beguiling.

Poesie Franco-Anglasie

Je m'apelle K., comment allez vous?
S'il vous plaît, c'est bon, merci beaucoup
If you good, that's all that matters to me,
I am thanking you.
No creepy glare or sleepy stare
Would compare to any rivalry
A cost I could not bear,
I prefer we be in ceaseless harmony.
C'est la vie
La mer de reverie.
Une belle vue qui fait fondre vous,
Oh oui!
Such is life,
A sea of dreams with views that make you melt -
None such as beautiful, as the sight of you!

PREVIEW

The Town Upon A Hill

K. Scott Fuchs

THE PARISH OF STANDISH

I shut my eyes and I am seated on the train, cold air blowing down onto my face from the vents, hissing and blowing into the carriage around me, threading the silence with a white noise that created an ambience unto itself.

This is a Northern Service from Manchester Victoria to Blackpool North, we've now arrived at Wigan Wallgate. Please exit the train to the left and take care when stepping onto the platform.

A beep sounds followed by the whine of the doors sliding ajar. My eyes open to the exit but none step onto the train, I recline back against the blue cloth of the headrest and listen as the clatters of foot traffic and chatter on the platform briefly fill the train before the beeps sound again and the train draws silent. I close my eyes as the train embarks and pulls down the track. A whoosh of wind hugs the sides of the train, banging against the windows, as it roars down the tracks. As I found myself drifting in and out of consciousness, my eyes flung open to a set of terraced new build houses overlooking a lush green field. They shimmered under the sunlight breaking through the white cotton ball clouds sprinkled across the blue summery sky. A lane wandered onward from beneath the arch that the train crossed, whizzing by an instant. However, this small estate seemed to have time sail around it, a world unto itself. What it must be like to be down there and take in the scenery, I thought. To bask in the wheat and tall grass, with oaks and willows at the end of the clearing in every direction.

Perhaps, I would never know and it would just be one of those places you see in passing, it was somewhere outside Wigan that's all I could infer; a place I would likely never visit because I never stumbled across it otherwise.

Who lived down there? An innocuous question with a seemingly open-ended answer that may never bring forth a conclusion. Years went by and I never thought of that small thatch of rural splendour again, until one day....

My eyes were glued to the white ceiling accented in shadows as the lights were off, my back aligned vertically atop my mattress, listening to the moans of the fan to drown out any dissonances from outside. It was easy to shut my eyes and drift off to sleep, that was what I had been doing for days, when I was unaware and blissfully at rest, I didn't think. And when I didn't think, I didn't have to dread nor did I have to feel the glass shards cut deeper into my chest. If I could get the energy to just get my feet to touch the ground and then free myself from this convalescence. I never wanted to lie down again, I wanted to walk, run, and dart around with vigour and jubilance. If I could move these legs with muscles turned to jelly, aching to stretch. I could go outside, take a drive, or perhaps have a smoke....

Was this it? Was this all there is? Does all of it mean anything? How many more days, weeks, and years will speed by like a high-speed railway car? These moments, all towns whistling by in a second without any opportunity to stop and take a look around. How did I know that I would not find myself back here again? With only more time spent and more energy expended? Was there even a point?

I rolled out of bed and sprinted toward the car outside, not even locking the door to my flat as I shut the large blue-panelled door shut behind me, the paint chips had started to peel off. I crossed the road and a car passed behind me as I took in the panorama of a shoppe on the corner and a Wetherspoon's hotel across from me. Patrons were scattered at various benches with beverages enbibed, chortling and guffawing with the occasional yelp of emphasis from more merry punters. The name, The Mesnes Arms fixed over the frontage of the premises.

The keys jingled in my pocket as I removed them to open the car door. A blast of heat wafted across me as I got into the firm upholstered driver seat. I turned over the ignition and placed a cigarette in my mouth. I sparked my lighter and turned up the radio before I put the car in drive and made my way straight ahead to the A49.

I passed through a roundabout following a green sign which pointed toward Chorley, a collection of old Victorian houses pitched back behind iron-wrought gates stood vigilant on both sides of the road, digging their heels into their position that they have remained for over a century. The area was called the Cherry Gardens and though it had been built up, it retained a level of bucolic splendour from the bygone era it originates from.

A sign followed welcoming me to Standish in Langtree, an owl decal centred in the middle. I veered right at a petrol station, empty with no cars in the queues. A series of Victorian terraced houses lined each side of the road, pitched back a bit to distinguish their class of owner. The houses soon faded into newer and larger brick builds with slate drives and swinging brass gates. Ahead of me the silhouette of Winter Hill reaching above the treeline with the top of the mast blinking red.

A post office passed on the left, a woman in a purple sweatshirt exited her black Peugeot with a mobile phone in hand, making a straight bolt for the door of the building. Further down the pavement, a white cat trotted along in the direction of a few tits pecking at some wrappers abandoned to the street. Three pre-adolescent girls sprinted in pursuit of each other, long blonde and brown streaks tailing behind them as they ran underneath another green sign which provided directions at the forthcoming roundabout: Town centre and the M6 to the left, Chorley and the A6 straight ahead.

The music turned over to *"The Opinionated are so Opinionated"* by Poison The Well, an arrangement of sound without words but it need not any lyrics: the melody spoke for itself and it fit the surroundings. A ubiquitous loneliness and gentle melancholy intermingled with a sense of serenity and comfort, as if the music itself was accepting that this was how it was going to be without any impetus to act: an acceptance of the end without any mention of the violent exertions undertaken to avoid such a fate. A town upon a hill whose gates were perceptible from the distance whilst collapsing on the road paces afield, never to know what it was like to gain entry after such a rigorous journey.

I passed through the roundabout and left Rectory Lane quickly behind me as the car ascended the hill past a sign on the left that read WORTHINGTON. The black Arial-font letters boxed in white with a matching black border serving as the final post warning that it was now too late to turn back. There that followed was a tunnel of love, the lane canopied in elm tree leaves which beckoned motorists onward toward bucolic splendour and rural serenity at the end of the rich green vacuum. It was a passing thoroughfare leading to Antoniette's, on the other side a dwindling light greeted travellers. Instead, I remained in the void. Nothing bright lay ahead only more pain; more agony; more suffering; the atmosphere was basted and steeped in heartbreak and shattered hope.

Telephone wires crossed over the road underneath sycamore leaves that dangled over Wigan Lane as it met a solitary oaken pole at the crest of the hill. The trees blanketed the lane until I passed a bed and breakfast nestled in the shade to my right. I pressed the down button on the window and took in the fragrance of peat and grass that lightly seasoned the evening air as I was suddenly surrounded by lime green farmlands on both sides of the road, the blackened tarmac with a double yellow line carving through the grassy fields serving as a counterpoint between the new and old. The only hills that were in view now were the darkened swells to the East, the antennae mast at Winter Hill now more fully defined standing vigil as it looked over all the Douglas Valley in front of it.

A red tractor rolled by on the road, perhaps a farmer on his way back from completing a run. I remember the black diesel tractor that continued to cross my rambles through Blackrod, the first night I met

Annie, wondering if he was stalking me or him equally concerned, I was following him.

The farmer in the tractor ahead of me drove past me in my old Volkswagen unbeknownst that I was anything more than another passing blur. It's funny how we never ponder what is going on in the life or the mind of the one who is heading in the opposite direction from us, as we travel: are they heading home or are they trying to find it? What are they returning from? What are they heading towards? This must occur a hundred or thousands of times a day, and we blissfully carry on unaware seldom to stop and think.

My musings were interrupted by another sign which was white with black font with a red circle that indicated a hidden road was half a mile away. The clockface of St. Catherine's Church in Blackrod peeked its face onto the horizon, long far in the distance. The structure of the tower was decorated at its top with St. George's Flag.

I remembered that first night in Blackrod when I stood upon that very hill and prayed as I glanced out to the passing red lights on the M61: this was a new beginning, please let it be the end of this loneliness; please let this be an answered prayer and what I was always waiting for.

Once again, I was on my own watching from afar, as I had always been. Annie and the girls: they were everything to me. But now, they were things of the past and I was nothing more to them than a sentence in a novel.

My attention turned to a final lay-by that hugged the right shoulder with a view into a wheat field beside it; a last bastion to bail out on the destination of where this journey led. But I was determined to finish what I had started.

I turned left at Platt Lane and the music turned off, a silence filled the car which matched the air of Standish. The tyres whistled along the road, serving as the only perceptible dissonance accented by an occasional chorus of rumbles.

No birds were cawing, cats mewing, or mufflers sputtering, just the rustling of rubber against tarmac as a faint breeze entered and echoed through the windows.

The clouds hung low and the sun bent beneath them, tinged in a golden haze as twilight approached. The fields grew extra tall and I passed the gates of the cemetery across from a row of terraced houses, the capstone dating to 1902.

How many have come and gone? How many years were spent on this road chronicling the growth and change? How much of it stayed the same?

100 years ago, families may have very well glanced out their windows at the same fields. A little girl sat in the top floor window in a ghostly white chemise glancing at a calendar dated to 1915, wondering what the world would be like 100 years from now. I was the response to her foresight. The world indeed may have been more advanced but the languish was all the same. People may live longer but that gives them more time to think about what they have lost.

Perhaps, eight years onward this girl who looked down from the first-floor window blossomed into woman-hood and she would excite at the thought of getting married, imagining and maybe even drawing herself dressed in a beautiful white dress with hair done impeccably on her day of nuptials; soon enough the day would come and as soon as she was there looking down on this road, so long ago, she was gone. But this place probably hadn't changed much despite another generation passing and another completed cycle of life.

I had dreams like hers once too: to be the man so blessed that The Lord would grant him the blessing to witness such a spectacle and be a part of it. I also had the dream to stand at the altar and watch my bride approach. Her smile concealed by a lace veil as I glanced up at the rafters of the church, wondering if what I was experiencing was real. The image of a baby in her arms flickering ahead of us, followed by a home of watching our scions romp about, reflecting back to the day it all started. I had that dream too and it died. And now, I had to die with it.

Of all the possibilities, timing, and intersection of metaphysical dimensions that needed to be purported for it to manifest, there was once a point when I was in the same room as Antoinette Collier, one whose beauty and grace could not be captured in mere words. I loved her from the moment, I saw her.

There was a day when I could behold her, hear her breathe, and smell her scent lingering throughout her house and now it seems I would never again. That day was no more and I could not bear the thought of a world where she existed but no longer existed in mine. The future ahead of me was now buried in the past; gone in a blink, arriving fast as it departed. But there was never any marker of it.

I made my way through the bend past the country pub on my left, recollecting the first time I travelled down this road as I went to Antoinette's house, recalling the butterflies floating through my stomach and the images of things not yet come true.

The long green meadow appeared, flanked by the car park to the pub, the lane I was travelling down, and the estate of newly built terraces on the far end. In the middle of the row of red-brick and brown-linoleum façade houses was her house. The heart-shaped wreath that she hung in her window, I reminisced of sitting on the couch and looking out the window at the field on a sunny blue day. The view had a much different flavour and persona as I watched the cirrus clouds float on by. As I neared the street, I pulled over and took in a survey of the scene. The line of oak trees at the other end of the field, extended around to the footpath that led onward from the estate of houses. Then, the fence and the incline toward the train tracks with the overhead wires held up my large metal gantries serving as sentries watching over all that passed through or dwelled within the area. Their arms held up the cables over the tracks, another daring feat of strength as they flexed their muscles to demonstrate their supremacy.

I turned the car off and reclined in my seat, leaving the battery on. I put on *Dreams* by The Cranberries and lit up another smoke. Listening to the song was like being with her, it was her favourite, after all. My hands brushed across the passenger seat, past a red rose resting on the seat over a few sheets of paper stapled together. I gently picked up the flower and slid the note out from underneath it, re-reading what I had written early in the day.

The cigarette dangled in my mouth as vapours of smoke danced through the car, their footsteps left in a silver haze that trailed their serpentine rhythms.

Dearest Annie,

I love you so very much, I am sorry...

A gust of wind roared as a train sped by on the tracks. The wind chased the train but could never catch it. The one that eluded so many, now in pursuit of something it could never touch. However, I never wanted to run. As the train went past, I watched each and every carriage pass on the trestle in front of me, thinking about the speed at which the vehicle was travelling, the force that it moved with, and what it would be like to see it barrelling down toward me. I squirmed at the thought, imagining the explosion of every joint, bone, and muscle of any human that would be pulverized by it at full velocity.

But as quick as the pain came, they would soon be obliterated. But how long? The agony may last seconds, minutes, or hours while blood sprayed in a mist that stained everything around it: the bushes, the trees, the branches, and leaves, layered in sanguine debris. Why suffer such a fate? Does it really have to ever come to that?

Such thoughts seldom crossed my mind when I stroked her cat, Tabitha who had a purr that sounded like a motor engine. A gentle orange and black ball of fluff that was sweet and gentle, I had never met such an affectionate creature. A smile filled my face as I remembered the days that Emma and Isla would storm through the door after school and rush to pet Tabitha who sat on the couch puffed up awaiting her younger sisters.

Both girls would gently run their hands along her back, their sandy blonde hairs down their back in ponytails over grey dresses and green undershirts. Their school uniforms added another element of unity to their sistership: incarnates of the daughters I always wanted, girls who became so precious to me...

I flicked some ash from the cigarette out the window, tears filled my eyes. Antionette's purple Nissan was parked at the gate to her front yard, where the girl's bikes and scooters rested gently on the green grass that gleamed in the faint glimmers of evening light. Purple...her favourite colour. A light turned on in a window above the front room, where the bathroom was situated. I observed from a distance all the activities of the house and imagined what they could be doing. Were they watching a movie? Were they playing hide-and-seek? Was she giving them a bath before putting them down for bed? I used to be a part of all of it and now I was on the outside looking in. They were no different than anyone else who lived in the houses beside them, I didn't know them and I was nothing more than a phantom; a ghost; a poltergeist, wandering in the moonlight trying to figure out what comes next and what has happened. Another gust, another train passed by in the opposing direction. My eyes once again fixed on the tracks. I took another drag and went back to reading more of the note.

We called each other soulmates but now that seems like a lifetime ago. Perhaps, I have already died and been condemned to Hell. On the day I first met you, I thought it was a new beginning but as it was written: the end of the matter is better than the beginning. I suppose even now such words apply, as this matter has to come to an end and these sufferings were meaningless. What has been is what will be and what has been done is what will come."

The words of the letter followed me with every breath and movement I took. All the years before her, battling this disease day-in and day-out to culminate in this? As it was written, there is still hope if you are alive. A living dog is better than a dead lion. Maybe she would have a change of heart; maybe she would come to her senses; maybe she would awaken from sleep and rush to her phone. And then the phone rang....it was her! My fingers scrambled as I pressed the green icon on the screen with excitement.

"Annie?" My voice filled with urgency to match the haste. "I've missed you!" The words could not escape me fast enough, their reverberations were still flowing through my chest cavity. I yearned to hear her Scouse accent, the seconds seemed like an eternity accent.

"As have I, Kevin." A sniffle muffled the air. "You've become a part of the furniture and it's not the same." She sniffled again. "I must see you, where are you, lad?" Her voice was warm and motherly as if she were calling me back home after being lost.

"Not far from you, actually..." My heart started to beat rapidly and a euphoria filled me. A tranquillity and a peace that embraced me with warmth. The feeling of stepping into a warm and illuminated house after spending hours out in the darkness and cold. A cosy feeling that felt like home, surrounded me again.

"Please call." She spoke with similar urgency. "We must have a natter about all of this; we can sort it out but we can't have this happen again." A smile filled my face and tears filled my eyes. "No, we can't." I sighed. "I'll be there in a minute..." I swiped a tear from my eye. "I love you, Annie."

"I love you more." The phone went silent again and as I looked at the screen again, I saw the call log in my phone tracing backwards to the date we split up: the last time we spoke on the phone before she had blocked me. I scrolled through the texts sent to that number that were never viewed or read, just one tick next to them dating back to that fateful day. I pressed the green phone icon to dial her again and it went straight to voicemail as it has. Nothing ever changed but for a moment, I pretended they had but the fantasy soon came crashing back down to reality. She was gone, she was never coming back...but I refused to accept it. I couldn't; I didn't want to let go.

Night had now fallen upon us. I left the note and the rose on the windscreen of her car. I took one more look down at the rear of her house, the lights were on her bedroom and kitchen as she remained unaware. The girls perhaps finishing their colouring at the rear kitchen table in their pyjamas as she made a cup of tea. The three of them safe in the house, a long way from where I stood though they were within viewing distance.

A buzzing filled the air, hissing louder and louder. I looked up at cables above me running parallel in a straight line, as a white light grew larger as it approached me. I never wanted to end up here, I feared the day but the eve was upon us.

In that moment, a series of images flashed in front of me: moments long elapsed recollected as if they were yesterday and other scenes not yet experienced, a series of alternative events that may happen or could have happened if things did not unfold the way they have. Grief consumed me followed by guilt and remorse, the buzzing hummed louder as a horn sounded, and the rails on either side of me whined as I watched as the light neared, remembering when I was a passenger on that train passing through here many moons ago....

More by K. Scott Fuchs

The Miss Temperance Lee Series

Don't miss out!

Visit the website below and you can sign up to receive emails whenever K. Scott Fuchs publishes a new book. There's no charge and no obligation.

https://books2read.com/r/B-A-HCTAB-OHMXE

BOOKS 2 READ

Connecting independent readers to independent writers.

Also by K. Scott Fuchs

Six Months in Wigan
Time and Temperance
Poetry From Ryecroft Hall
Mrs. Coleman of Coalbrookdale
Waiting for July
Sycamore Grove
A Day We Met In Lynbrook
The Town Upon A Hill

Watch for more at www.kscottfuchs.com.

About the Author

K. Scott Fuchs is a novelist, published poet, actor, and performer. His debut novel *Time and Temperance* was released in 2023 along with *Six Months in Wigan,* a collection of poetry. He is also the author of *Mrs. Coleman of Coalbrookdale,* (the prequel-sequel to *Time and Temperance),* *Poetry from Ryecroft Hall,* and the forthcoming novel *Sycamore Grove,* the third novel in The Miss Temperance Lee Series.

Please visit **www.kscottfuchs.com** or contact K. Scott Fuchs at **kscottfuchs@gmail.com** to join the mailing list or for any other inquiries related to both novels and poetry releases.

Read more at www.kscottfuchs.com.

www.ingramcontent.com/pod-product-compliance
Lightning Source LLC
Chambersburg PA
CBHW021121130726
47988CB00003B/1108